Previous Publications:

Everyone's Alone Tonight (with Jason Baldinger)
(2019 Kung Fu Treachery Press)

Things Have Changed
(2019 Dark Particle Press)

The Park (2019 Aldrich Press)

Against the Dark: road poems (with Tyler Robert Sheldon)
(2019 Stubborn Mule Press)

Little Fires Hiding (with Jason Baldinger)
(2018 Kung Fu Treachery Press)

You've Heard It All Before (2017 GigaPoem)

As I Watch You Fade (2016 EMP)

Jack of Diamonds (2013 LAB 52)

Flight 776 (2012 LAB 52)

From the Back

Poems by

James Benger

Kansas City, Spartan Press, Missouri

Spartan Press
Kansas City, MO
spartanpress.com

Copyright © James Benger, 2020
First Edition1 3 5 7 9 10 8 6 4 2
ISBN: 978-1-952411-23-6
LCCN: 2020938517

Cover and title page image: Jon Lee Grafton
Author photo: Hannah Benger
All rights reserved. No part of this publication may be reproduced or transmitted in any form or by any means, electronic or mechanical, including photocopying, recording or by info retrieval system, without prior written permission from the author.

Contact:

jamesbengerauthor@gmail.com

https://jamesbenger.wordpress.com

https://www.facebook.com/james.benger.3

https://twitter.com/JamesBengerKC

The author would like to thank the *365 Poems In 365 Days* poetry workshop, the members of which were repeatedly pummeled with early versions of these poems throughout 2015, John Dorsey and Jason Ryberg at *Gasconade Review,* and Tasha Roberts at *In Between Hangovers* for giving many of these poems their first life, Jason Baldinger for writing a couple books with me, where two of these poems originally appeared, Brandon Whitehead for his constant support, Jeanette Powers for giving an early version of this book an honest read, Alarie Tennile, whom I really should've thanked before for helping me score a publisher for the last book, and Dad, Hannah, Milo and Felix for all the obvious reasons.

TABLE OF CONTENTS

From the Back / 1

Aftertaste / 3

Venom / 5

Another / 6

Transplant / 7

beginning / 9

The Upside / 11

Caged / 12

Standards / 13

Correspondence / 15

Shuffle / 17

Etiquette / 19

The Only Way / 21

Faded / 23

Potential / 24

Seeker / 25

Everyone Pays / 26

The Hunter / 28

Fly / 30

Habit / 32

The Cure / 33

Everyone's Alone Tonight / 34

Post-Gig / 36

Hope / 38

The Calling / 40

Insular / 41

Party of Two / 43

Living the Dream / 45

Optimism / 47

Lower / 48

Flowering / 49

Above / 50

As always, for Hannah, to whom I owe everything.

The piano has been drinking, not me.

-Tom Waits

From the Back

I sit in this dark corner,
watching it all happen.
Another drink poured,
another one spilled.
Another advance
rebuffed,
another temporary couple
leave with hands in
each other's back pockets.

I sit in this dark corner,
and wonder why I do this.
It serves no good.
In the long run,
the joint loses on
soft drinks.

I'm not doing anyone
any good.

But still,
I end up here
every night.
pad on table,
recording the
minutia of
mundanity.

Some of the long-timers
have faded off;
here every night,
then just gone.

New ones come
nearly every week.
They'll all be part
of my record,
the record of
my life
recording
their lives.

Aftertaste

What's left of the
green plastic
army man who
drove a truck
in Germany is
slouched over the bar.

In the dim lighting,
it's hard to tell if
he's awake,
asleep, or
more than asleep.

A fourth or fifth
glass of bourbon
neat sits in front of him,
the rim dangerously
close to his slowly
sinking forehead,
threatening to impale him
like all those near-miss
Nazi bullets.

He drinks alone every night,
surrounded by intoxicants
and the intoxicated,
all packaged and sold
long after his first
physical war ended.

He stirs, looks distastefully,
distrustfully at the glass, then
repeats the narrow-eyed
grimace when he catches a
glimpse of himself in the
mirror behind the bar.

Nothing tastes the same
as it used to.
Nothing but bourbon
and grudges.

Venom

He spouts his truths,
another highball down.
His crowd ebbs and flows;
the rhetoric draws crowds,
but they quickly become
bored with the tediousness.

A one track narrative of
the great evil around the corner.
The preacher at the opposite end
points his finger and
spits the same venom.

Another

She came through that heavy
door with the smudged glass
so she could leave it all.

Glass after glass,
conversation after monotonous
solitary, she finds herself
no less frustrated,
no less alone than before.

Her days get her down, but
her nights keep her here with us.
If she could only hit the bottom, then
she could work her way back.
If not to the top, then to somewhere
closer to living than this repetitive
undead waking nightmare of existence.

The creep at the dartboard likes the
way the barstool cradles her ass.
She orders another.
Nothing new will come tonight.

Transplant

She came here with
all the hopes and
good will an early
twenty-something could.
Her eyes reflected the
neon signs in a way that
only youthful exuberance
can.

She moved here for him,
and as that story usually
goes, he didn't stay.

At first it was something
to do, somewhere to
meet some new people,
build some kind of
lasting connection,
some tie in her quickly
unravelling ball.

She used to come here
on Friday nights, or maybe
at five on a weekday, if it
had been particularly horrendous.
Now we see her every night.
Close to tears, she's gone
home with half the bar.
The lights no longer
bounce in those eyes.

beginning

he does everything right,
exercises every day,
goes to work,
pays his taxes,
loves his dog,
volunteers at the
      soup kitchen on holidays,
gives the guy on the corner
      a dollar,
reads the paper,
votes his conscience,
doesn't go to church, but
      doesn't look down on
            those who do,
gives out full-sized
      candy bars at halloween,
            even to the kids who
                  are really on the high end
                      of young adult,
buys local,
recycles,
when he has to drive,
      it's a hybrid
lives alone, but isn't lonely…

at least that's what he tells himself,
but he ends up here alone
      every night,
one turning into three,
a pitcher into two,
the bartender tells me
      our man was here in the
           middle of the day yesterday,
this beginning has been
      a long time coming.

The Upside

She leaves like she came:
alone, sad, but hopeful.

The cool, sweating glass
feels like home in her palm,
and she'll never admit how
much she enjoys the attention.

She found reasons to
not come back,
but she found even more
to keep the stool warm.

Caged

I keep getting split-second
glimpses of him,
stained shirt and sad eyes.
The door swings on its
weighted but unbalanced hinges
and at its most open,
I see him.
He soundlessly prepares the
greasy bar food for the
drunks and drinkers,
a flit of a small radio
momentary overtaking the jukebox.
I watch for each swing
of the door,
hoping to catch some new
element of his existence.
Over a carelessly carried
plate of fried pickles,
I catch his eyes.
His pupils emote a
wordless desperation.
Then the door swings shut.

Standards

He's been sitting at
the table near the
front door for hours,
nursing a now warm and
mostly flat pitcher.

From his vantage
point, he sees them
come and go easy.
He does this most nights;
has them sized up
before they've ordered.

Tonight he's got his
eyes on the brunette
at the pool table in back.
He's watched her shots
go from impressive trick,
to adequately playable,
to where they are now;
borderline amateur.

He guesses two more
and she'll gladly give
him her keys and
off they'll go.

He'll never know
her name and
tomorrow she won't
remember his face.

Their actions won't be
disinfected with the same
pleasant precision
as her inhibitions.

Correspondence

She's got a white lace
handkerchief that she's repeatedly
pulling out and dabbing at
her glistening forehead;
the booze sweats have
already set in.

She'd be pretty if it weren't
for all the tears running the
once heavy makeup.

She started with fluorescent,
presumably fruity drinks, but
she's long since switched to
double shots of tequila,
no salt, no lime,
chased with a Diet Coke that
hasn't touched her painted lips
in three shots.

She's crying,
and drinking,
and sweating,
and writing
a long, long something.

It started with deliberate,
dainty curls, each one
punctuated by motionless thought,
but now the words come
fast and hard and violent.
She grips the pen
like an icepick.

She wipes her head again,
yellow, stinking sweat,
motions to the
man behind the bar
for another round,
then goes back to
etching hate into paper.

Before the next drink comes,
between violent letters,
she mutters:
"Fucker,"
or maybe it was:
"Father."

Shuffle

Nietzsche said something about
an hourglass being flipped over
again and again and we're all
just grains of sand forever
lost in the shuffle.
A sad concept, a
play on Socrates and
in places like this,
the only absolute truth.

The couple at the
table in the middle,
with their bleached smiles and
matching designer hiking jackets,
they don't belong here,
everyone knows it, including them.

They order craft bottles and
clink the brown glass in
laughs and smiles and a
good cheer that is more than
foreign to the lackluster lighting
and peanut and vomit floor.

Unlike most of the others here,
they have a future to go with
their past, and their present
is more water than mud.

After tonight, I'll never see
them again, their adventure
continuing far past these
wood paneled walls and
spiderwebbed windows.

For me, they are just another grain
about to be lost forever in the shuffle.
For them, I'm not even that.
That which is lost, still exists,
but in their world,
I never was, and
never will be.

Etiquette

There's only one urinal, one toilet,
and it never fails that
every time your back teeth
are really floating,
you're better off heading to the
alley out back.

I'm bleeding the dragon
against a frozen brick wall,
humid ammonia cloud
rising like the noxious smoke
from a fire at a munitions plant.

The scurrying in the dumpster
on the other side of the alley
I'd dismissed as rats turns out to be
a greying man, roadmap skin and
dull-to-the-point-of-dead eyes.

Some of the nicer patrons
will piss in used beer bottles
instead of using the wall.
They leave them lined up,
freezing to the pavement.

The man gets from the dumpster,
picks up a bottle, tips it to his mouth.
There's an equal chance it's beer,
or piss, or cigarette ash and spit.

I zip up and go back inside.

The Only Way

He finds it difficult to
experience anything real.
The neon technicolor of life
burns hotter than the cigarette
lighter in the dash of his
blue smoke and spent prayers
'76 Buick Century.

He could've known love once,
maybe even did for a breath,
but as always, anything vivid
frightens him to collapse.

The young waitress in the
skirt that's tight enough and
short enough to get any kid
sent home from school,
she sets his next glass on
the table and tries to
flirt for a bigger tip.
He mumbles a terse thanks,
never looks her in the eyes.

He'll go home tonight,
numb and alone; not
necessarily the way he likes it,
but the only way he knows.

Faded

Hard to believe
she was a beauty queen,
a model student,
a star athlete,
etc…

Hard to believe,
impossible, really,
but the conviction
she spits in her endless,
countless recountings
of her youthful
exploits in the
world of up-and-comers
almost weighs heavier
than the whiskey drool
running down her
sagging chin.

She'll leave tonight with
someone who will
treat her rough and wrong,
someone who'll
leave without words.
Then tomorrow she'll be
back to tell us all again
how she could've had it all.

Potential

Under the awning, cigarettes glowing,
the patrons convene with only the
percussive music of the midnight rain.

Boozy scents swept free by the autumn breeze,
couples in arms, acquaintances in deep discussion,
life on a somewhat corrected keel.

Windows behind backs rattle from within,
streetlamps flicker with no promise of dawn,
yawns hidden behind callused, overworked palms.

Outside reminds us of what life could be.

Seeker

The place is open all day,
though it tends to be
pretty dead until quitting time.

She started coming in around
two, desperate stories of
a job interview that
might pay off.

Each day that she
shows up earlier, the
hopeful stories of the future
grow dimmer and the
hateful diatribes of the
past gain destructive momentum.

Today when she showed
up at nine, the bartender
asked her if maybe she'd
want coffee instead.
She actually considered it,
if only for a second.

Everyone Pays

The owners stopped trying
to run him off a while ago.
Most of the regulars find him
at least tolerable, the tourists
looking for a little bottom-shelf
adventure see him as quaint,
some even go so far as "whimsical."

He's never made enough to
buy a hard shell case, so he
unzips his frayed gig bag,
lays it on the sidewalk and begins.

He whips around Bob Dylan
and Joan Baez, doubles back
to Blind Willie McTell,
shoots forward to Connor Oberst,
always hinting toward something
new, something entirely his own.

He tried to let himself in once,
but it only takes one hard
brown bottle to the forehead to
drive oneself back into oneself.

After a particularly hoarse set,
he came in and asked for water
one slippery August night, but
nothing is free, everyone pays
for everything.

The Hunter

Even when desperately trying
not to, the whole bar
can hear his endless, boundless
self-aggrandizing babble.

Backwards ball cap and
pitchers of Bud Light,
counterfeit dog tags threatening
to choke out the flow of
his bulging jugular,
small sleeveless shirt on
a medium frame to accent
what tone there is to show.
Eyes constantly darting to
the ass of the jailbait with
the fake ID at the dartboard.

As the collection of empty
pitchers on the craggy, sticky
table continues to increase,
the conversation devolves from
half-baked, ill-informed politics,
to the merits of modern country music,
to high school football,
to a literal dick measuring contest.

When there's no room left on
the table to place another round,
he pushes his chair back and belches,
long and grotesque, louder than the juke,
stands and walks over to the
dartboard, self-consciously
flexing his tattooed biceps.

From where I sit,
I'm not sure if my stomach
is telling me a need to vomit
or cry.

Fly

She woke this morning
with puke on her chin
and piss in her pants.
Not the most successful night,
but not the worst either;
she did get her party on at least.

Last night she made the rounds
until every table, every
available stool was
no longer friendly to her;
needy drunks, no matter
how well meaning, are
tedious, even to other
needy drunks.

Only the bartender would
listen to her tragic woes
draped in a cocoon of
false frivolity.
He wouldn't've,
but even bartenders
need to earn beer money.

So as the staff was mopping
the floors and dreaming of
their personal lives,
she was stumbling
(and for a few sad seconds,
crawling) back to her
apartment, three blocks away.

She passed out on the living
room floor, keys still in the
wide-open door.
She'd wake to wet pants and
a crusty, sour mouth.

She's back tonight,
a million dollar smile
and a story to tell.

Habit

She used to come here
on those Fridays that
capped off an armageddon
of a terrible week.
On those evenings, it was
a weak martini that
saw more absent swirling
than actual drinking.

On this Friday, I've seen
her here every night.
Remembering a time when
she wasn't parked at the bar
promptly at 5:15 pm is a challenge.
The ever present martini is
still in front of her,
grown stronger and
punctuated by shots.
The job and the life
has grown no harder,
but the habit has.

The Cure

It was coming out
both ends all last night,
and most of today.
At least once,
he passed out sweating
on the bathroom floor.
Fever dreams of sobriety
were nothing more than that.

By the time the sun had
died he was back here.
He's convinced himself
that alcohol of any form
will beat any disease,
kill any germ.
He's almost fooled himself,
but despite his best efforts,
he will wake up tomorrow,
and all other tomorrows
alone and sick,
until he
doesn't wake up at all.

Everyone's Alone Tonight

There's too many people
alone here tonight.
Almost no conversation,
unless you count
waitresses and bartenders
angling for high-test tips.

The girl by the door,
she keeps making the move
like she'll leave as soon as
this last one is drained,
but the next one comes
before she can,
stuck in an endless loop of
just one more…

The old man at the bar
is more than hunched over
his infinitely refilling
shot and beer,
the way his head droops,
the liquid will outlast him.

The wiry man in the back booth
slowly nods his chin down to his chest,
bouncing back up,
barely touched pitcher vibrating
on the scarred table.
He shuffles to the can,
comes back a few minutes later
a new man,
runny nose, red eyes
and a can-do attitude.

Everyone in this place is alone tonight,
even the old man in the back room,
half-chewed cigar like some cartoon trope,
sorting the cash, the checks,
the crippling credit card receipts,

Everyone's alone tonight,
and this place won't fix it.

Post-Gig

They played an exceptionally
good gig tonight,
people yelling and jumping,
so now, after the club's
closed, most of the crowd
has gone back to their
real lives, he's here,
shot after shot after shot.

He was supposed to follow
the guys back, help unload
the gear back into the practice
space, maybe help setup for
the morning jam that will be
just a few hours from now.
They gave up waiting on him
a few hours ago.

They played an exceptional gig,
despite the fact that he was often
a little off, not quite in tune, and
a bit fluid with his timing.
Muddy club acoustics, no one
but the audiophiles in the crowd
caught on to his subpar performance.

He didn't either, or didn't care,
already well on his way to the
floating joy of the bottom.

He's at the bar, buying shots
he can't afford, a girl half his
age wrapped in either arm.

The guys have already decided
if the morning's jam doesn't go well,
he's out, already a replacement in mind.

They played an exceptionally
good gig tonight,
and floating on the waves of everything,
no one can tell him otherwise.

Hope

I've seen him before;
he does this a lot.
Pacing the block,
hand on the door,
then backs away,
almost comically,
practically making a
cross with his fingers.

He spent every night
here for so long,
I was sure he'd be stuck.

But he's trying,
trying.
Some nights he wins.
Few and far,
but some nights he does.
I suppose that's what
keeps him going,
keeps him hoping.

The streetlights blink
into life, and his palm
is on the door.
I hold my breath until
he walks away for
another lap,
talking himself up
to talk himself out.
I hope he wins.
He's working at it
hard enough,
he deserves to get out.

The Calling

She blanks and
the calling comes.
She wishes it was
the guitar or the
milk carton or
even a fucking
coloring book, but
it's always, always
the bottles, sitting,
not a speck of dust,
more clear glass
than brown,
calling,
calling.
Tomorrow she'll
go without, she
promises herself
as her mouth
waters at the sight of
it splashing into the glass.

Insular

She spent most of her
Saturday in bed.
Not sick, physically,
but violently ill at
the thought of going
out and seeing the
sun, the people.
The trees with their
healthy green mockery.
The cheerful finches
who's song assures her
that she is the only
one who feels this way.

Beneath blankets, the
tormentors still come,
but at least they come
from within, and there
isn't an audience of
strangers to witness
her demise.

Five pm brought the
only thing that could
force shoes on her feet
and movement in her legs:
the glass bottle in the freezer
was all but empty.

She wouldn't be here if
this place wasn't between
her apartment and the store.
She needs some courage
to face the clerk because
he knows, he sees just
how broken she is,
and she can't take any
more sympathetic,
judgmental, pathetic eyes.

Two more and she should
be good to buy her
replacement bottle and
crawl back into herself.

Party of Two

They come here most nights,
the two of them with nothing
else to do but sit and drink.

They justify that this is better
than doing the same thing
at home on the couch,
it's better than sitting
across from one another
at a silent dinner table
staring at their phones
or their books,
but most of all,
it's better than being sober.

Nearly every night they're here.
The glasses of red wine stack up
and before too long, what would
be a painfully quiet night at home
becomes a jubilant celebration
of living,
and of each other.

They'll leave in each other's arms,
content and in love,
saved from a threat of
unlubricated silence.

Not all the stories
end in tears.

Living the Dream

It's part of the routine,
part of the workweek.
Eight hours
(nine if you count lunch break)
in a factory he's
tired of but familiar with,
doing things that at this point,
require pretty much
zero thought.

When the swipes his card,
gets into his rusted out T-Bird
and holds his breath,
praying to the ghost of
Henry Ford that the engine will
kick over, instead of the
pitiful death rattle it sometimes spits,
that's the moment when he lies
to himself, says that this is
where real life begins; the past
over-third of the day was
just some nauseating
waking dream.

He gets here,
nearly same time,
always same seat every day.
Before he unloads in his
corner booth, the one with the
knife cuts in the faux leather
from some long-forgotten indiscretion,
his first pint is poured and
on its way.
You can tell how bad the previous
hours' waking nightmare was
by how many more pints follow.

He sits alone and nurses his beer,
doesn't dare go home to the
lonely, quiet emptiness of the
house that all his sleeping hours bought.
He waves up font for another.
He says this is where real life begins.

Optimism

Taking a sip from her
barmate's can, she tells him
that thing's aren't as
cool as they used to be.

She might be right;
the can's been sitting untouched,
getting steadily warmer,
no condensation left on the
outside of the aluminum.

Her companion reminds her
that warm beer breath
never was cool.

She shrugs, calls for another one.
When it comes, she drains
half in one go.
"Better," she says,
"but still sucks."

For some, that's the best
the future can offer.

Lower

Dark far corner,
behind the pool table,
the video golf and
Deer Hunter games,
opposite the bathrooms,
no one comes by,
no one notices.
That's what he wants.

The air is stiff and hot
Even the bare bulb above
his booth has expired,
leaving him,
pickled though he may be,
the liveliest thing,
really the last living thing,
in that corner of the world.

As the reluctant waitress
brings him another
bottom shelf double,
when he ordered a triple,
he muses on the virtue of
lowered expectations.

Flowering

She sits with her sketchpad.
Corner booth, little light,
shouts and strobes will
not disrupt her art.
Dribbles of gin on the coaster
under the mostly untouched glass.
Her pencils fly with a weightlessness
unknown and forever unnoticed
by the regulars who mill about.

The crack of another ball
on its way to the pocket,
another line in her masterpiece.

I wonder why she comes here
to this chaotic maelstrom of
malicious uncreativity.
Then I look to my own paper,
my own pen.

She flies on the current of
her pencil.
In a knifed-up booth
in a rundown bar,
something beautiful is born.

Above

His latest round dead and drying
on the pitted table,
he stumbles to the juke,
pays his quarter to hear
the only Mingus in at least
a fifty mile radius.

Those first dissonant notes
send him into a head-bobbing,
finger-snapping, grinning fury
which takes him all the way
back to his seat.

He only opens his eyes to
catch the waitress,
motion for another,
then he's back on it.

The mood in the room shifts
to something lighter,
more real,

or maybe less real,
but nevertheless brighter,
more hopeful.

For a few short minutes
in this darkness,
everyone feels the sun.

James Benger is a father, husband and writer. His work has been featured in several publications. He is a member of the Riverfront Readings Committee and is on the Board of Directors of The Writers Place in Kansas City, and is the founder of the *365 Poems In 365 Days* online poetry workshop and is Editor In Chief of the subsequent anthology series. He lives in Kansas City with his wife and children.

www.ingramcontent.com/pod-product-compliance
Lightning Source LLC
Chambersburg PA
CBHW030138100526
44592CB00011B/943